T0166326

flourish

practical ways to help
you thrive and realize
your full potential

CICO BOOKS
LONDON NEW YORK

Published in 2021 by CICO Books
An imprint of Ryland Peters & Small Ltd
20–21 Jockey's Fields   341 E 116th St
London WC1R 4BW   New York, NY 10029

www.rylandpeters.com

10 9 8 7 6 5 4 3 2 1

A CIP catalog record for this book is available from
the Library of Congress and the British Library.

ISBN: 978-1-80065-016-9

Printed in China

Commissioning editor: Kristine Pidkameny
Senior editor: Carmel Edmonds
Senior designer: Emily Breen
Art director: Sally Powell
Head of production: Patricia Harrington
Publishing manager: Penny Craig
Publisher: Cindy Richards

contents

Introduction 6

introduction

Do you feel you are just getting by—surviving rather than thriving? With a wealth of advice and practical ways to increase your energy and drive, this book will help you be the best version of yourself: happy, healthy, and fulfilled.

In the first chapter, Nourish Your Body, learn how to boost your physical health through the pillars of wellbeing: movement, diet, and sleep. Discover how to find the exercise that's right for you; consider not just what you eat but also how you eat; and focus on creating the right conditions for better rest. The second chapter, Nurture Your Mind, helps you uncover how you work best, whatever your work may be, as well as how to find maximum enjoyment in what you do. Finally, the last chapter, Make It Happen, is about identifying your life's purpose and passions, and manifesting your dreams to achieve your goals.

CHAPTER 1

NOURISH YOUR BODY

shape up for happiness

Exercise is good for you in more ways than one. It tones your body, keeps you healthy, and boosts your mood, which in turn helps self-esteem and self-confidence. And let's face it, when we feel good about ourselves, we feel happier too, which leads to a positive frame of mind.

Exercise also triggers physiological changes within the body and the release of "happy hormones." Science tells us that those people who exercise at least two or three times per week experience significantly less depression, anger, and stress than those who exercise less frequently or not at all. If you are feeling a bit low, a quick 20-minute burst of exercise can change your mood and raise your happiness levels. Those who do battle with depression are encouraged to exercise for 30 minutes per day for a minimum of 3–5 days each week. Controversy remains about whether exercise leads to improved mental well-being, or whether those with positive mental well-being are more likely to exercise—but for anyone non-medical, the message is the same:

Exercise makes you happier.

why not try...

- Taking an exercise class? Not only will you learn a new skill, but also it will encourage and support you, and it's an opportunity to meet new people.

- Incorporating walking into your journey by parking the car further from your destination or getting off the bus or train a stop early?

- Taking the stairs or walking up an escalator?

- Giving the dog an extra walk? If you don't have one, could you borrow one from a neighbor?

- Walking around the block?

what exercise do you do at the moment?

Take a minute to reflect and write down what you already do. This might include walking to the store or with the children to school, or perhaps you are on your feet all day at home or at work. Include any form of movement that you do in your day. You might do more than you think.

However, if you find that you do very little exercise or if you would simply like to do more, start to think about what you could do. What is stopping you? Notice any thoughts that arise. Explore the resistance if it feels particularly strong. It is always better to start small and build up your capacity gradually—just adding a few extra steps a day can set you on the right path. The various digital trackers that count steps and other activity can be a good incentive.

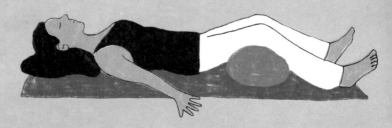

Many activities can be adapted if you have limited mobility (yoga is a particularly good example), but always discuss your needs with an experienced practitioner. It's important that any exercise is suitable for your age and health. If you haven't exercised for a while and you have health problems, do consult your physician first.

Exercising outside has the added benefit of allowing you to get a dose of fresh air and connect with the natural world.

exercise you could try

- Swimming
- Walking
- Tai chi
- Qigong
- Running
- Yoga
- Pilates
- Cycling
- Dancing
- Spinning
- Gardening
- Ball games
(tennis, badminton, netball,
baseball, cricket, football, squash)

where energy
flows, energy goes

exercising mindfully

Exercising can be a great opportunity to integrate mindfulness into your everyday life. Any activity can be done mindfully, and the underlying principle is always to know what you are doing while you are doing it.

The following description of how to approach this is for running, but the principles are the same for any activity. The instructions are not a step-by-step sequence. All you need to remember is to check in to the head (thoughts), heart (emotions), and body (physical sensations) regularly throughout the activity, and notice what is arising.

be aware of how it feels in the body.

• Notice your breathing—is it fast, slow, or labored? Are you holding your breath, perhaps? Notice how you respond to whatever you notice. If your breathing is labored, the story might include some self-judgment ("I'm so unfit") or perhaps anxiety ("I'm going to have a heart attack!"). The instruction is always just to notice the story and how it feels in the body. Staying as grounded as possible in the physical sensations of the body will help to prevent unhelpful thoughts from spiraling out of control. Remember that it is okay to stop and rest, and it is important that you do so if you feel unwell.

• Notice your posture, paying particular attention to any areas of tightness or tension. Are your shoulders raised? Are your hands clenched, or your jaw? Simply notice how the body reflects your state of mind. There is no need to actively try to change what you notice, although often when we become aware of tension—say in the shoulders—it will release naturally.

• Notice the physical sensations of running—the feet in contact with the ground. Which part of the foot makes contact first? What follows? Remember, we are not thinking about the action of running, but simply noticing it.

Scan through the whole body from time to time.

notice what is going on in the mind.

Your body may be running through the park on a beautiful morning, but is your head already at work? When you notice that your attention is pulled away from the present moment (even by positive things), just bring it back to noticing the moment and what is arising internally as well as in the environment.

become aware of any emotions.

There might be frustration, peace, calm, disappointment—name them, and be curious about whether there are accompanying, connected sensations in the body.

expand your awareness.

From time to time, take in the environment around you—the sights, sounds, and smells. Drink them in. Notice which ones you are drawn to and which you recoil from. Can you identify a sense of liking or not liking in the body? Where does it manifest? How does it feel? Be as specific as you can.

notice your attitude.

It is also useful to notice what attitude you are bringing to the activity. Does it have a driven quality? A sign of this might be if you are focused on how fast or how far you have run, or how many calories you are burning. When we do something mindfully we are more interested in what we are experiencing in each moment than in an end goal. This often means that we relax; paradoxically, this can improve performance, but that is not the aim.

exercising with others

It is easier to exercise mindfully by ourselves, simply because we can focus exclusively on our own experience. If you are running and chatting with friends, for example, all your focus will be on that interaction. There is nothing wrong with this, and exercising with friends is a great way to support one another as well as to have fun. However, you may choose to do the activity on your own from time to time, so that you can practice it mindfully, or—if you are with others— just practice mindful awareness for a few minutes every so often.

Some types of class, for example a high-impact aerobics or spinning class, will be more challenging because of the pace, but you could still experiment with tuning in to the head, heart, and body from time to time, or even just before and after the class, and reflecting on your underlying intention and attitudes.

When we are working out with other people, it can also be interesting to notice whether our comparing mind kicks in—are we faster, slower, fitter, thinner, fatter than the person next to us? We may be judging ourselves or someone else, but either way, the invitation is simply to notice the thought—"There I go again"—and bring the attention back to the body and any physical sensations that may be arising.

energy foods

To get through a busy day, we all need a brain that is sharp and focused, whether as kids going to school, adults at work, or simply in order to play a fun game of chess with a friend. All day long, the ability to concentrate for a prolonged time can be a challenge, especially as life for many of us is fast-paced and involves ongoing interaction with brain-stimulating technological devices. What we eat and when we eat directly affects how well our brain functions—and that is empowering to know. Our brain needs a steady stream of energy from food for optimal cognition, memory, attention, happy thoughts, and stable mood. It can use glucose from carbohydrates, such as grains, vegetables, and fruits, or amino acids from various proteins, such as cheese, meat, or eggs, for energy, but it prefers various fats as a long-lasting source of fuel. Try to build your diet around foods that provide a large variety of nutrients and brain-supporting fats and oils. Your body needs the best if you are to enjoy a life of vitality, productivity, and joy.

top 20 foods for energy, mood, and focus

- Dark leafy vegetables, such as spinach* and kale

- Purple grapes

- Multicolored berries

- Avocados*

- Coconut oil

- Free-range egg yolks*

- Extra-virgin olive oil

- Wild salmon (smoked, cooked, or canned)*

- Rosemary

- Turmeric

- Gingko tea

- Green tea extract

- Brahmi tea

- Grapeseed oil

- Walnuts*

- Cod-liver oil

- Butter*

- Dark chocolate*

- Navy (haricot) beans

- Pasture-raised meat

Some foods are starred: if you find these foods do not improve your energy, mood, and focus, you may be suffering from a sensitivity to them—consult a health practitioner for advice.

power up with breakfast

All day we need energy—and our brain does, too. Breakfast is the most important meal (or drink) of the day; after all, it really is a call to "break" the "fast" after our sleep. But it also matters how we manage the notorious mid-afternoon slump, when there is a natural dip in cortisol, our daytime hormone.

Breakfast greatly affects our blood sugar. It determines whether we will enjoy good concentration for learning or performing at work, or suffer funky moods and lack of focus. What we eat and drink within the first hour of waking matters greatly.

For a productive and high-performing day, include a good source of protein in your breakfast. A lack of protein in the diet affects our blood-sugar balance, mood, and concentration.

try these breakfast options:

- A bowl of creamy goat yogurt with organic blueberries (sweeten with stevia if you wish) and ground flaxseeds

- A fluffy mixed-vegetable omelet with a slice of multigrain toast, or sautéed vegetables on the side for a gluten-free option

- A bowl of yummy oatmeal (porridge)

- A fruit smoothie with added avocado or protein powder

mindful breakfast

What is your breakfast routine? Do you stop long enough to nourish yourself? If you do eat breakfast, how do you eat it? Are you reading the newspaper, checking your work e-mails, or making sure the children have everything they need for school? We all lead busy lives and, if children are involved, breakfast can often feel like a battleground, but if that is the case, how does that make you feel?

Experiment and observe the differences between your normal routine and a breakfast routine that incorporates mindfulness. Decide which you prefer. Even if it is not possible to do this every day, perhaps it is possible to do it once a week or at the weekend.

• For a few days, pay attention to your breakfast routine. Notice what you do and how you do it. Notice how you feel immediately afterwards. If you haven't eaten breakfast at home, do you pick something up on the way to work and, if so, what is it? Perhaps you eat breakfast at work—how does that feel?

• Now make an intention to eat your breakfast mindfully. Remember that any activity can be done mindfully by intentionally paying attention to what you are doing without judging it. When you notice thoughts intruding, simply bring your attention back to preparing or eating your food. Food is more than just taste—explore what you are doing with all your senses—the colors and textures, as well as the smell. Savor them.

• If you are eating breakfast at work, you can still eat it mindfully. It might not be ideal but if that's all that is possible for you to do at this point, then that is good enough. Start where you are.

• It is a misconception that we need more time to do an activity mindfully. What can happen though is that when we become interested in the activity, we slow down and linger over it longer than we normally would. So perhaps allow yourself the luxury of a bit of extra time to do this, if possible.

• As before, notice how you feel during the activity and immediately afterwards.

• Compare the two ways of eating breakfast, and, if you have found it helpful, explore how you can introduce mindfulness into your everyday breakfast routine.

lunch and munch

In Mediterranean cultures, lunch is a family meal, and some people even take a siesta afterward. Taking an afternoon nap is not common anymore, but it is still important to be mindful of how we fuel our brain and maintain optimal blood-sugar levels in the afternoon. This includes taking the time to sit down, without being distracted by technological devices, and shifting our presence and gratitude to the food in front of us. Such foundational points can be most difficult in the busy lifestyle of the twenty-first century, but giving the brain a time-out from multitasking is very helpful. It facilitates improved digestion and the absorption of nutrients that allow us to function at the highest level.

The midday meal can be hearty, because our digestive power is strong—yet it is at this time that we tend to eat on the go, or perhaps even skip lunch altogether, as other commitments demand our attention. The brain becomes stressed if we do not break properly to eat, and that will affect our mood and outlook on life.

A drop in blood sugar can lead to tiredness in the afternoon; protein for lunch lifts our mood and keeps our focus sharp.

try these lunch options:

- A hearty bowl of beef chili or mixed vegetable soup
  (particularly if you live in a cold climate)

- A salad filled with a colorful variety of vegetables, nuts,
  and goat cheese

- Sesame chicken wraps

got that mid-afternoon sinking feeling?

The mid-afternoon slump is a complaint of many. It is then that sugary treats such as cookies or candy, coffee, cigarettes, or caffeinated sodas can be tempting, because they provide instant fuel for a tired brain. They are not good for long-term alertness, though, not to mention health, so instead, when the pangs strike mid-afternoon, try something that is not sugar-filled to give you a boost.

try these snack options:

- A yogurt smoothie sweetened with stevia or raw honey

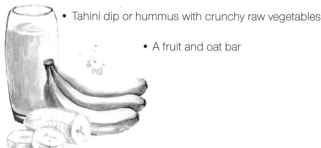

- Tahini dip or hummus with crunchy raw vegetables

- A fruit and oat bar

consider your dinner

Whatever you choose for dinner, it should always involve high-quality ingredients and rainbow-colored foods that each have their unique healing properties. Begin with a salad or a small bowl of soup to get the digestive juices flowing. For the main course, pair a portion of protein with fresh and seasonal vegetables for color and taste. And why not entertain your taste buds and stimulate visual delight, not to mention improving your gut flora, by adding a condiment of fermented vegetables, such as sauerkraut or kimchee?

try these dinner options:

- Chunks of sheep cheese with an interesting array of greens, beets (beetroot), and quinoa—a lighter option

- A grilled sea bass with dark leafy greens and sweet potatoes with parsley

- Rosemary shish kebabs

- Chicken tikka masala

how much dinner, and when?

Some people prefer to enjoy a small dinner, feeling that a heavy meal in the evening affects their sleep. Traditional Chinese medicine holds that it is best to have a large breakfast, a good lunch, and a smaller dinner, as the digestive fire is not so strong in the evening. The traditional Indian system Ayurveda also suggests that it is best to eat dinner before 7 pm, so that we can digest it before going to bed.

At night, while we are asleep, our brain needs a steady supply of blood sugar so that we can get a good night's sleep. It is important to note that everyone is different; if you experience hypoglycemia at night, it is a good idea to experiment to find what works best for you. Some do well with a small protein snack before bed, such as a little hard cheese and nuts, or a few tablespoons of yogurt. Others do better with a carbohydrate snack, such as unsweetened applesauce with a teaspoon of coconut oil and stevia. Pay attention to how hungry you are at night once you start eating regularly during the day. Listen to your body and see what you crave—the body does not lie.

dessert: yes or no?

There is a place for a little sweetness in our lives and on our food
plate; after all, it has healing properties that are well described in
Chinese medicine. Naturally occurring sugars provide sweetness
and have toning and relaxing properties, and also enhance the
function of the digestive system. Moderation is key: a little sweetness
from naturally occurring sources goes a long way. If you want to lose
weight, save dessert for special occasions only. Even a coconut
macaroon after a meal, or a piece of organic dark chocolate with
a cup of licorice-root tea, can satisfy a craving for sweetness.

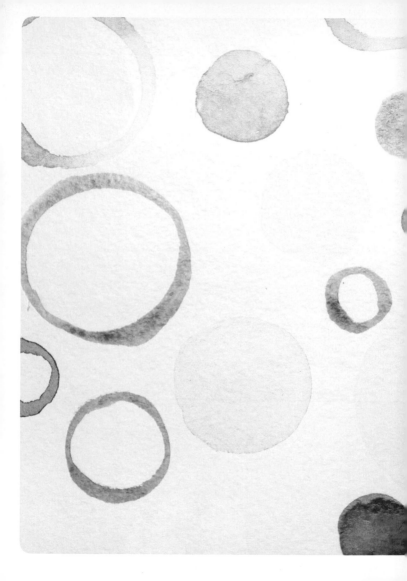

you deserve
good things

sleep well

It's often said that diet, exercise, and sleep are the three foundational pillars to good health and well-being. While many of us understand the importance of eating a healthy, balanced diet and of keeping fit, we are perhaps less familiar with how important sleep is.

We spend about a quarter to a third of our lives asleep, but just because we are not awake doesn't mean that time is unproductive. The physiological changes that occur when we are asleep determine how well we feel and perform when we are awake.

We've all experienced the effects of too little sleep: what it means for our mood, focus, and concentration, and also how it affects us physically—we have less energy, and feel tired and groggy. However, the importance of sleep and the consequences of being sleep-deprived go beyond this.

Sleep influences all the major systems in our body, and those systems in turn influence our sleep. Insufficient sleep can disrupt bodily functions that affect how we think and behave, and how we think and behave can disrupt our sleep. Therefore problems with sleeping can quickly become a vicious cycle.

sleep plays an important role in:

- Creating a healthy immune system

- Repairing muscle

- Consolidating learning and memory

- Regulating growth and appetite through the release of certain hormones

- Regulating mood and emotion.

Sufficient sleep is essential to our well-being, both physically and emotionally, so it is not surprising that when we are deprived of it we feel the impact in all areas of our life.

DID YOU KNOW?

Sleeping in a cooler room is helpful in facilitating the natural drop in body temperature that will encourage the onset of sleep.

how much sleep do we need?

There is no "golden" number of hours that is the perfect amount of sleep, and subjective sleep quality (whether we feel we have had a good night's sleep or not) is as significant as duration. Two people can sleep for a similar amount of time with similar periods of wakefulness, and yet perceive it very differently. In general, eight hours is usually quoted for adults; children and young adults will need more and the elderly less. However, it is important not to get too hooked on numbers, particularly if you do have trouble sleeping, since there may be a tendency to constantly measure how you are doing and then feel disappointed if you are falling short. This may create additional anxiety about sleeping, and that is unhelpful. Taking a mindful attitude to sleeping helps us to let go of particular expectations and of striving toward a particular goal, and instead helps us to be okay with the way things actually are.

ask yourself the following questions
after an average night's sleep:

- Do I feel healthy and happy?

- Do I depend on caffeine to get through the day
  (particularly first thing in the morning)?

- Do I feel sleepy during the day? (This is usually a sign
  that you are not getting enough sleep.)

Depending on your answers, you may decide to make
sleep a priority in your life.

your ideal amount of sleep

Try one of these practices to work out the number of hours' sleep that is best for you. Before you begin, pay off any sleep debt by getting plenty of sleep. You may need to do this while you're on vacation!

if you have a set wake-up time

Using 7½ hours as a starting point, count back from the time you need to get up and make that your bedtime (factor in a short period of "falling-asleep time"). Begin going to bed at that time for at least a week or, better still, ten days, and notice whether you begin waking up just before your alarm. If after ten days you still need the alarm, go to bed a little earlier and continue until you find the right duration for you.

if you have the flexibility to get up at any time

Go to bed at the same time each night and notice when you wake up naturally, without any outside interference. Doing this over a period of a couple weeks will allow you to determine how much sleep you personally need.

The test is sleeping for a particular length of time and waking naturally (without an alarm) feeling refreshed, without needing any stimulants such as caffeine. However, you may want to have an alarm clock set as a back-up!

For some people, it's not just the duration that matters but the timing. Night owls and early birds may have to change the time they go to bed in order to accommodate that, and that will affect when they rise (assuming they still want to achieve their particular ideal duration). As always, have some fun experimenting with what works for you.

sleep questions

why are some of us "night owls" and others "early birds"?

Our internal body clock, or circadian rhythm, is set to approximately 24 hours. However, if your clock runs faster than that, you are more likely to be an early bird and wake up early. Night owls' clocks run more slowly, and they prefer going to bed later. Although we may have a genetic predisposition to be one or the other, we still can exert some control. For example, if you are a night owl who has to get up early for work, employing good sleep hygiene habits (see page 48) will help to override your natural tendency to stay up late, ensuring that you are not short-changed on your sleep.

is napping helpful?

Be aware that if you suffer from insomnia, napping may make it more difficult for you to fall asleep at night, and may thereby exacerbate the situation. In many cultures, an afternoon siesta is built into everyday rhythms, often as a practical response to a hot climate. Many people report feeling more alert and rested after a nap, and it can be a good way to pay back some of your sleep debt, but the key is to keep it short, ideally no more than 20 minutes. Nap for much longer and you risk falling into deep sleep, which may leave you feeling groggy when you wake.

can we catch-up on sleep?

Many of us try to make the most of the weekend or days off by lying in to catch up on sleep. However, this may not be helpful, because it disrupts our body clock. As we get older, our ability to sleep in and catch up on sleep is much reduced. It is much better if you can stick to your usual time of getting up and going to bed, even at weekends.

WAKING NATURALLY

You can buy daylight alarm clocks that mimic the rising sun, gradually increasing to full strength at the alarm time. By using light to wake ourselves up, we are tapping into the body's own internal systems regulated by the circadian rhythm. This can be a much gentler and more restful way to wake up than a strident alarm call.

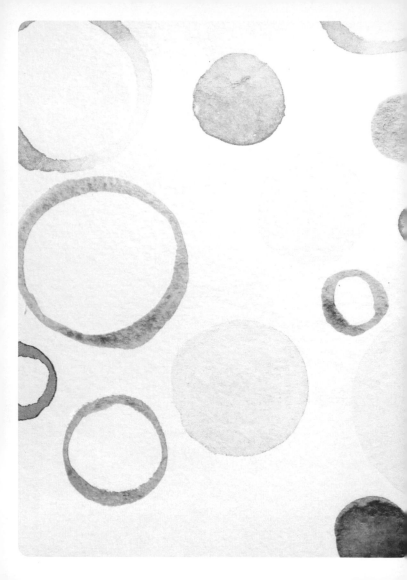

sleep is that golden
chain that ties health
and our bodies together

THOMAS DEKKER

the effect of technology

For most of us, the days when bedrooms were simply places to sleep and make love are long gone. First it was the appearance of the television, then the smartphone, laptop, e-reader, and tablet. All are now commonplace in our bedrooms.

There is nothing wrong with the technology or the objects themselves. It's simply that the presence of these items immediately signals activity—doing something—rather than resting or letting go of activity. Also, the way we engage with them can have a negative impact on our sleep.

A smartphone, laptop, tablet, or television screen acts as a mini sun, emitting blue light that interferes with the production of melatonin, a hormone that is essential for becoming sleepy. While on some phones it is possible to activate a nighttime filter that reduces the blue light, it doesn't remove it entirely.

The gadgets themselves are a source of distraction. Checking emails and status updates on social media keeps us in a state of hyperarousal. The brain remains on alert for what might pop into our inbox or social media feed, rather than being encouraged to wind down in preparation for sleep.

Using a smartphone for work keeps us connected mentally long after we have physically left the office. It becomes harder to disconnect from work during the evening, and that can lead to rumination that disrupts sleep. If you work from home, it is even more important to give yourself a mental break by making a clear distinction between work and leisure hours.

Notifications and alerts can interrupt our sleep. Healthy sleepers will experience up to ten brief arousals or awakenings per hour of sleep. These usually last only seconds, and they are often associated with body movement. Their fleeting nature means they are usually forgotten, and so we are unaware of them unless they are prolonged because of a sound or other factor such as smell. If an alert sounds on your phone during one of these mini awakenings, you are more likely to wake up properly. If you are someone who experiences problems with sleeping, this can set off the reactive pattern of insomnia.

good sleep hygiene

There are some simple changes we can make to ensure that we are supporting rather than undermining our body's internal sleep systems.

cool down

Body temperature plays an important role in sleep. We fall asleep as our body temperature drops, and a lower body temperature also helps us stay asleep before it begins to rise in the early hours as we waken. You can encourage a drop in body temperature deliberately by taking a hot bath or shower about an hour before bedtime and then making sure your environment is cool (about 63°F/17°C). As the body cools, you will begin to feel sleepy. Ideally, exercise no less than 4 hours before going to bed, to avoid elevating your core temperature.

environment

Sleep in a cool, dark room that is free of technology and has a comfortable bed. Turn any clocks to the wall to avoid watching the minutes in the early hours.

keep to a regular schedule

Stabilize your circadian rhythm by going to bed and getting up at the same time—even at weekends and when on vacation.

don't spend too long in bed

If our mood is low, we may retreat to bed rather than face the world. However, going to bed too early means repeated awakenings and a much shallower sleep, and we thereby miss out on the restorative section of sleep.

listen to your body

If you cannot sleep and are awake in bed, be awake. Read, get up, meditate, or do some yoga or other calming activity.

notice what you eat

Certain types of food eaten too near bedtime can affect your sleep, but
they can affect everyone differently, so pay attention to what you eat.
Avoid stimulants, too: alcohol, caffeine, nicotine, and other stimulants
are best avoided in the evening and perhaps
even in the afternoon.

reduce screen time

Avoid screen time (including television
and cellphones) an hour before bedtime,
if possible.

protect your wind-down time

Notice what helps you to move from the busy-ness of the day to winding
down toward bedtime. Avoid, or keep to a minimum, activities that keep
you buzzing. However, notice if there is a sense of striving when it
comes to doing particular activities or behaving in a particular way, with
the expectation that they will lead to a good night's sleep.
This is unhelpful, too.

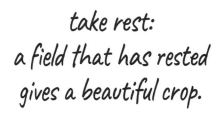

take rest:
a field that has rested
gives a beautiful crop.

OVID

wakeful nights

Lying awake at night can be stressful. We might wake up thinking about work, and then thoughts about being awake intrude and start a spiral of anxiety. The easiest way to disengage the thinking mind is to turn our attention to the body. It is important to let go of wishing for a particular outcome. Remind yourself that by doing any of the three practices on pages 52–57 you are resting the mind, and if the mind rests, the body rests.

watching the breath

• Lie on your back with your feet falling apart and become aware of the body in contact with the bed. Perhaps begin by scanning the body from the heels all the way up along the legs, buttocks, back, neck, and head. Just notice how the body is held and supported by the bed. Allow yourself to be supported. Let go of any sense of "holding on." Take a deep breath in and let it out.

• Place one or both hands on your belly and drop your attention to the palms of the hand. Become aware of the contact of the hand with the belly and begin to become aware of the breath, and in particular the out-breath. You may find it helpful to say "out-breath" silently to yourself each time you become aware of it, the hand gently falling as the belly contracts and the breath leaves the body. Notice how the body responds to each out-breath. Allow the body to let go of the out-breath completely.

• Just continue watching the breath in this way. After a while, you may find yourself watching both the in- and the out-breath equally and that's fine.

• If, at any time, thoughts intrude about "not falling asleep" or other worries, just label them as thinking, gently remind yourself that you are simply breathing without any expectation of falling asleep, and escort your attention back to the out-breath (we can do this over and over again). Regardless of whether you do fall asleep or not, being with the breath in this way will settle the mind and you will feel more rested.

breathing through the body

In a half-awake state, you may not be alert enough to judge what practice to choose or how to do it. The following is perfect for just that state of semi-consciousness and can also be done while wide-awake. Doing this will help you tune into your body more quickly and easily, and when we focus our attention on the body we disengage from our thoughts. If we do this when we are still half-asleep, we are more likely to keep our thinking mind at bay.

- Lie flat on your back and imagine that you are breathing in through the soles of your feet. As you breathe in, the breath travels up the legs and through the torso and as the in-breath turns into an out-breath, you are breathing out through the crown of the head. Continue in this way for as long as you wish. What we are doing is allowing the breath to sweep through the body in a regular rhythm, entering and exiting the body.

- Remember that we are not doing this in order to fall asleep. If you do, that's a bonus, but it is important to let go of that expectation, otherwise every second or so you will jump out of the body and back into your head, measuring how sleepy you are (or not) and judging the experience. This is what we are trying to let go of.

counting breaths

Counting sheep is a time-honored way to fall asleep, but whatever object we choose to focus on, the mind will often come up with inventive ways to distract us. We can minimize this by bringing two techniques together—counting and turning our attention to the body. We can do this by counting breaths.

- Find the place where you can feel the physical sensation of breathing most strongly, commonly the belly, the chest, or around the nostrils/upper lip. It might be helpful to place your hands on your belly.

- As you breathe in, count one, then breathe out. On the next in-breath, count two, and so on.

1 2 3 4 5

• Continue counting up to ten and then start again at one. If you go past ten, at the moment of realization, simply break off and return to one. You will often go past ten. Remember that we are practicing bringing the wandering mind back, so the more we do this, the greater the exercise we are giving that "muscle of awareness."

• The neural pathways for thought and exploring physical sensations are the same, so the body can only do one at any one time. Although our mind will always wander, we are making it harder by focusing on a bodily sensation rather than a thought such as sheep. We use a limited count so we know when we have wandered away and where to come back to.

6 7 8 9 10

deep sleep

Yoga nidra is the centuries-old yoga practice of deep sleep. It can be quite a long practice, of about 45–50 minutes in length, and is easiest done listening to someone guiding you. There are numerous recordings available on the Internet for free or to buy. The following practice follows the same principles as yoga nidra. It is simple to follow and thus easy to remember, so if you can grasp the basic principles, it is something you can do without relying on any external devices.

• Lie on your back, with your arms and legs outstretched, feet falling apart, and the hands a little away from the body. Take a few moments to connect with the body by lightly focusing your attention on the breath.

• Become aware of the right side of the body. Bring the right side of the body into awareness: the right foot, leg, arm, and torso, all of it.

• Let go of the right side of the body and, in your mind's eye, bring the left side of the body into awareness: the left foot, leg, arm, and torso. Picture the whole of the left side of the body.

- Let go of the left side of the body and, for a minute or two, become aware of the entire body, from the toes to the top of the head, from the tips of the fingers to the length of the back. Hold the complete body in awareness.

- Now let go of the complete body, and become aware only of the body below the waist. In your mind's eye, become aware of the feet—the heel, sole, and toes of each foot—and the lower legs, knees, thighs, buttocks, pelvis, and belly. Hold the lower half of the body in awareness.

- Let go of the lower half of the body and become aware of the top half of the body—the area above the waist: the back, shoulders, arms, and hands, the back of the neck and the head. Hold the top half of the body in awareness.

- Let go of the top half of the body and become aware of the entire body lying here.

- Now imagine that the body has been segmented horizontally, becoming aware of the back of the body, the area that is in contact with the bed or floor. Move your attention around and notice the points of contact or the absence of contact.

- Let go of the back of the body, and become aware of the front of the body. Imagine the area above that horizontal midline—the face, the chest, the belly, the front of the thighs, and shins.

- Let go of the front of the body, and become aware of the entire body—the torso, the limbs, the front, back, and sides. Rest with the entire body in awareness.

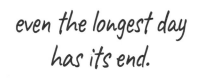

even the longest day
has its end.

IRISH PROVERB

CHAPTER 2

NURTURE YOUR MIND

getting to know your brain

We are all familiar with the concept that if we over-exercise, we will get physically exhausted. Most of us would avoid planning a day packed full of physical activities as we know our body's limitations. However, we don't usually think about our brains in the same way. Yet the pre-frontal cortex—the area of the brain that deals with decision-making and other higher-level functions—uses up a lot of energy compared to more routine activities, such as those done on autopilot.

When the brain's resources are depleted, it will resort to more automatic ways of thinking as this takes up less energy. When we are on autopilot, we are more likely to fall into habitual patterns of thinking and behavior, and these are often unhelpful. Old ways of thinking are also not going to give us the new strategy we need to bring the latest product to market or whatever project it is that we are working on.

If we accept the idea that our higher brain functions are a limited resource, we can begin to think about how best to use them. In *Your Brain at Work*, David Rock emphasizes the importance of this. In order to conserve the brain's resources, Rock recommends:

• Scheduling activities according to the degree of attention they require. Therefore, the start of each working day should be spent "prioritizing the prioritizing" as this involves a large amount of decision-making.

• Holding multiple tasks in one's head at any one time is exhausting— two to three is our ideal limit, but the fewer the better. Therefore, writing down your to do list for comparison will use up less energy.

• Think about the different activities you do throughout your day (dealing with e-mails, phone calls, meetings, managing others, talking to customers). Schedule those which require a greater degree of concentration or decision-making for when you feel fresh. Bear in mind that if you are working on something new or creative, it will require more brainpower than something that is more routine-oriented.

• Grouping like-minded activities together will make better use of your brain's resources than repeatedly switching back and forth between different types of activity, which becomes distracting.

• Remember to factor in some downtime to allow your brain to rest and reboot. Downtime might be a routine task, such as tidying your desk.

Notice how your attention ebbs and flows through the working day. Make a brief note of different activities, the time of day, the degree and length of time you felt focused, and any other observations. Do this for a week, so you can determine any patterns in terms of your attention (or lack of it) versus performance.

Begin to implement some of the above strategies, using the information you have gathered about your brain and your average working day. Bring the same attitude of curiosity and experimentation to this stage—what do you notice about working to make best use of your brainpower?

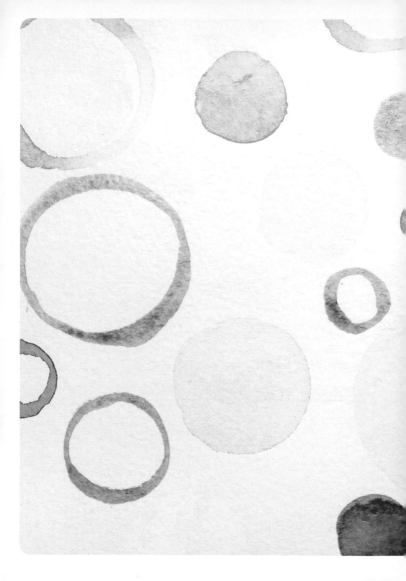

knowing others is
intelligence; knowing
yourself is true wisdom.

LAO TZU

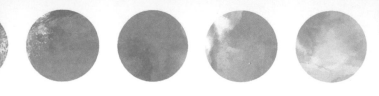

curiosity

Children are inherently curious. As we grow older, things we encounter become more familiar and we often take what we experience at face value. If we have been in a particular role at work for a while, or with the same company, we get used to a certain way of doing things. We put up with systems and models that can be clunky because "that's the way we've always done it." When someone new comes along, they tend to be more curious and question the status quo, or perhaps suggest a different way of doing something. Is there any reason we can't bring that kind of curiosity to our existing job now? When we explore something with curious interest, we often discover things we were unaware of—this may be physical sensations, emotions, or motivations, and we might even notice things about other people.

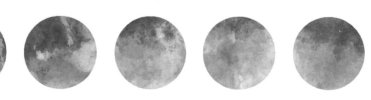

• Today, be curious about everything. Assume no foreknowledge and explore your world of work. Ask questions without expecting a particular answer. Talk to people with whom you would not normally converse. Pay attention to the environment and how your colleagues interact with one another and the outside world.

• Be interested in your own experience. Notice what arises, and pay attention when there are moments of resistance—a sense of tightness or tension, which sometimes shows up in particular areas of the body. Where do you hold your tension? Are there particular people or tasks to which your body responds negatively?

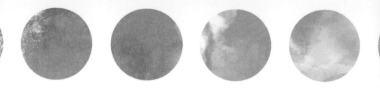

• What do you like? Pay attention to those moments when there is a softening, an opening, and a moving toward something. When do you notice this? Are there particular activities, foods, beverages, or people that cause this? Is it in response to something that you do?

• Pay attention to specific e-mails, phone calls, and conversations—notice if at any point your body gives you a physical reaction and notice what happened just before. Be interested in any associated thoughts that arose just before, during, or after this reaction. Do you notice any particular emotions? Sometimes there are more than one.

• Pay attention to the feedback that your inner self is giving you via the body. Notice whether there is a contradiction between your thoughts and physical sensations or emotions in your body. Sometimes we find ourselves agreeing to do something or assuring someone we are "fine," and yet at the same time there is a clenching in the gut or a tightening across the shoulders that suggests things are anything but fine.

• Be curious about what you discover about your experience and how you act at work.

reach your potential

It's easy to put a cap on our own abilities, believe we are only proficient in one area, or view our abilities as finite. When we put a limit on ourselves, it immediately shrinks our potential and stops us from taking chances. The following exercise can help you to address any long-held beliefs you have about yourself that may be limiting your potential.

For this meditation, you will be observing your own reflection and you can sit or stand in front of a mirror. To improve our belief in our own potential, we have to deal with the very person who is placing limits on what we feel we can achieve—our own self.

1 While standing or sitting in front of a mirror, take a few moments to center yourself so you feel calm and focused. Look at yourself in the mirror, not in the superficial way we often regard ourselves (noticing a hair out of place, observing a line, or fretting over a particular feature), but looking at the person that strives, achieves, struggles, sometimes disappoints, loves, laughs...Think of all you have been through and the strength it has taken over the years to get to where you are today, and now look at yourself through these eyes.

2 Focus on a particular long-held belief you have about yourself, whether you think you can't communicate what you want and need or feel afraid to take the next step.

3 Ask yourself what it is that is holding you back. Be honest here; this meditation is just for you, so there is no reason to contrive an answer. Once we acknowledge our worries and concerns, we can then choose either to live with them or take the necessary steps to change things. Make a commitment to yourself to start making small steps toward changing this limiting belief. If, for example, you feel worried about asking for what you want in your work life, commit to beginning to tackle this situation, which may mean simply opening up to those around you so they know your needs and can give you the necessary support to start making those changes.

4 You can finish the meditation with a positive affirmation that, when spoken with intent and conviction, can help you reiterate to yourself what it is you really want and empower you to believe you can achieve it. Just remember to keep the affirmation positive and confident; you have to feel you are already living what you want so, for example, you could say: "I am working toward and achieving my goals" rather than "I hope to" or "I would like to."

This meditation can be used whenever you need a confidence boost. Remember to look at your reflection with compassion at all times, making sure that the affirmation is positive and encouraging.

going with flow

Mihaly Csíkszentmihályi (pronounced "me-hi cheek-SENT-me-hi-e")
has had a huge influence on our understanding of what it means to
be happy through his work on a concept he calls "Flow." He is one of
the world's leading experts in the field of positive psychology. When
we are in flow, we stop feeling conscious of time because we are so
absorbed in the task. The results of our work seem to come through
us rather than from us.

the conditions needed for flow include:

- A sense of being involved in the task.

- A feeling of being outside the bounds of everyday reality.

- A sense of clarity and focus—we know what we are doing and where we are going.

- Taking on tasks that we have the skill level to complete.

- Having the discipline to concentrate on what we are doing.

- A sense of timelessness—of being so involved that we are not aware of time passing.

His work has clarified that for a task to be satisfying, it needs to be challenging, but within the scope of our abilities. If there is too much stress involved, productivity diminishes; if it is too easy, the motivation to do the task drops. Flow is the opposite of apathy—it drives us to act with purpose. When we are in flow, our sense of self is suspended, although completion of the task reaffirms self-value and provides a sense of satisfaction for work well done.

start now

don't procrastinate

Procrastination is a major enemy of happiness because it will never allow you to plan ahead with confidence, relax without guilt, or produce your best work. Procrastinators miss out on parties, vacations, tax breaks, and even having children, because their dread of deadlines means they haven't been paying enough attention to how they prioritize their time. The art of chronic delay is worry dressed up as fear and accessorized with avoidance, pain, and guilt. Any pleasures in the life of a procrastinator feel stolen surreptitiously, because wherever you are and whatever you are doing, you know you should really be somewhere different, doing something else instead.

Chronic procrastinators feel full of self-loathing because they know they disrupt other people's lives with their delays. In letting others down, they let themselves down. Whatever the original cause (and there are many different reasons), the underlying problem is the strong belief that they can never be anywhere or get anything done on time. Of course, that is far from the truth.

making a schedule

"To do" lists are torture for a procrastinator, because they seem to get longer and longer every day, but a well-planned schedule can become a thing of joy and a route to happiness:

• Buy or print a one-page year planner so you can easily count the weeks and days throughout the year at a glance.

• Look around your home or your place of work, and make a list of all the things that you have started, but not finished. If you feel yourself procrastinating at the very thought of starting, just write down one thing. If you are serious in your quest for happiness, choose to do this now.

• Next, think about when you would like (or when you need) to have completed this task. Circle the date on your year planner.

• Work backward in your mind through the various tasks and stages that you will need to complete in order to achieve your end goal. Think

about this in stages, according to the complexity of the task. Think of a realistic time span for each completion stage, and then repeat the exercise, doubling the amount of time you initially thought was necessary to complete each one.

• The chances are, if you have already been procrastinating, that the date you come up with was some days or weeks earlier than today's date, telling you that you should have started by now and you are behind already. Normally, you would panic at this point and choose to do something else, as a diversion. Instead, tell yourself that you now have three choices: to arrange to extend the deadline; to ask someone to help you to deliver on time; or both. Sticking your head in the sand and pretending that time is malleable is no longer an option.

• The final step is to create a schedule—preferably using color to bring it to life. It will be best to devise your own layout, in a way that matches the needs of your task and the way you think. Draw it, create it in Excel, but map it out in such a way that you can pin the printed-out version on your wall and see it all the time. Set up reminders in your online diary if it helps—but the trick is to have something in front of you as a visual reminder of what actions to take at every moment of every day.

Two important points are worth bearing in mind. First, do not use the actual deadline as your scheduled deadline. Make sure the deadline that you list on your schedule is a good two weeks (or more) ahead of the formal cut-off. This is the golden rule. If necessary, leave the real date off your schedule altogether, so your brain is not distracted by it.

Rule number two is to highlight your start dates in a brighter color than your finish date, and tick them off as you go. Most schedules are focused around completion dates, which for the procrastinator is no use at all.

Once you discover the joy of completing tasks in good time or on time, your belief in yourself will slowly change—and you will have time to be happy on your own terms, too.

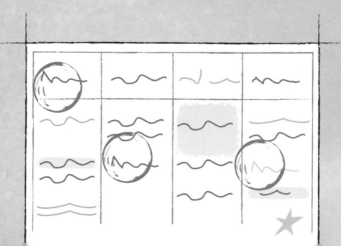

do everything today
with intention

technology detox

Staying connected with the workplace when we are out and about can be helpful. However, we can easily become a slave to our smartphone. This is particularly true during out-of-office hours or while on vacation. We may think that just "checking in" has little impact, but every time we do so we are turning our attention towards work. When we are mentally "at work" we are not present, wherever that might be. This impacts negatively on whoever we are with as well as on ourselves. Often our behavior has become so habitual that our experience seems normal. We can't remember when it might have been different.

try the following experiment:

• Decide when you can legitimately and reasonably expect to be "off duty" and make an intention to reclaim this time for yourself.

• Change the settings on your phone to turn off or remove a particular e-mail account. Some phones can be set up to do this automatically at a set time each day.

• Let colleagues know that when you are out of the office, you won't be checking e-mails or available for phone calls. If there is resistance to this, negotiate a time-limited period during which you will check in.

• Pay attention to your experience—notice any sensations of "wanting" or "resistance." Notice how your mood is affected as well as any effects on those around you.

• Be prepared to experience some resistance from yourself (as well as others) to this, but be persistent and stick it out. If you are struggling, begin with shorter periods, such as evenings and weekends.

• Notice how you feel when you return to the office after giving yourself a technology detox.

if only...

It is seductive to think that if our circumstances changed, all would be well and life would be perfect. However, the more time we spend daydreaming about being somewhere else, the less we pay attention to our job here and now.

Daydreaming creates a sense of dissatisfaction with the present and then we zone out. When we are not present, we miss opportunities. These might be chances to interact with colleagues or do something differently. At the most basic level, we are not present for a large part of the working week. Weeks become years and years build into a lifetime. Not being present at work can easily become a habit that we carry home with negative consequences for our family. Paying attention to the present moment with an attitude of curiosity creates an environment of discovery. When we pay attention, we become interested; when we are interested, we discover all kinds of hitherto unknown aspects of our life and the people around us.

try this exercise:

• Create the intention to notice whenever your thoughts wander off into the fantasy world of "if only."

• Whenever you become aware that you are daydreaming of the future, bring yourself back to the present by paying attention to your breath or the placement of your feet on the floor (see page 96).

• It can be helpful to label your thoughts as "daydreaming" at this point of realization.

• Keep doing this—letting go of any condemnation or judgment about where you have been or the fact that you have been daydreaming.

multitasking

Multitasking is often applauded. We answer the phone while signing letters or carry on a conversation with a colleague while finishing an e-mail. However, these activities all use the same neural circuits and become overloaded when we try to do too many things at once. Our brain works best when actions are done sequentially.

Performance benefits from focused attention. When we pay attention, we notice things both internally and externally, and we are able to have a greater awareness of what is going on. When we do more than one activity at a time, we are constantly switching our attention between competing tasks. Our attention is split, which causes us to miss things and negatively affects our memory, as every time we come back to one task, we have to get our working memory up to speed again. This takes time and is mentally exhausting because our brain has to work a lot harder to get the same results. This uses up energy, so our productivity declines a lot more quickly and we are more likely to make mistakes as our memory is impaired.

• Notice how you feel when you multitask and how it affects your work in the moment.

• Become aware of when you are multitasking and, if possible, pause, gently reminding yourself that you are trying to do something different.

• Multitasking is a habit, so it will take a bit of time to change. Don't be too hard on yourself when you forget—rather, celebrate the times when you remember.

• If you have to multitask, mix the tasks wisely. Combine a task that uses the pre-frontal cortex—the thinking brain—with one that is more routine-oriented. Routine-oriented tasks are "learned" and have become automatic and embedded in the basal ganglia of the brain. We can do these tasks without thinking, so they take up less energy.

the tyranny of perfectionism

We are often our hardest taskmaster—demanding more and expecting higher standards than we would ever dream of asking of a colleague. The bad news is that you are never going to get there—you will always feel as if you could have done better or worked harder.

This constant judging of oneself and falling short of expectations is exhausting and undermines one's confidence and self-esteem. Often we want everything to be perfect as a way of keeping control, but life, and particularly life at work, is always beyond our control. As we feel control slipping away, we work harder and demand more of ourselves in an attempt to keep hold, but it is like running on a treadmill that someone has turned up to full speed—we can run faster to keep up at first, but at some point we will trip up.

Begin to pay attention to those moments when you feel pressured. Perhaps it is about delivering a particular project or maybe it is a constant feeling when you are at work.

- What thoughts are on your mind?

- What stories are you telling yourself about this task and your role in it?

- What emotions are present?

- What physical sensations are arising?

Be curious about when you notice this behavior arising. What do you discover? Is it linked to particular tasks or periods at work? How do you behave toward others when you are feeling this way? How do you behave toward yourself—do you ease off or press the accelerator to achieve more? How does it affect you outside work—your sleeping and eating patterns and your social activities? How often do episodes like that happen at work? Perhaps keep a note for a week to see what patterns may arise.

Once we deliberately begin to bring a particular behavior into our awareness, we are in a much stronger position to do something about it. So if we can become familiar with this pressured quality and how it feels, we are more likely to notice it as it begins to emerge. This is the point to take action—to pause and notice it, turning your attention to what you are experiencing. Notice in particular the thoughts—and what is driving you—and perhaps challenge or reframe them.

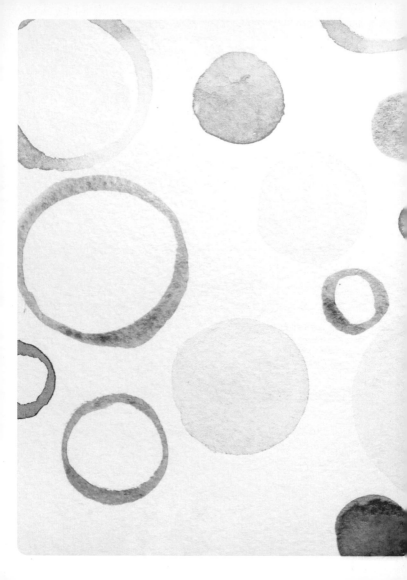

happiness is found
when you stop
comparing yourself
to other people

feet on the floor

This is one of the simplest and most useful practices to do when things are feeling particularly stressful and difficult.

When we are panicking, our breath becomes shallow and fast, making it difficult to turn our attention to the breath: the breath may feel elusive and awareness of this only makes us feel worse. When we feel like this, the best thing we can do is to ground ourselves by connecting with the earth beneath us. We can do this most easily through our feet.

Turn your attention to the feet. Do it now. Feel the sensations of your feet in contact with the floor. Push down slightly through the bottom of the feet. It is as if your feet were glued to the floor. The ground is solid beneath your feet. Explore these sensations—perhaps a sense of "shoe" or "sock." Wiggle your toes if you'd like to.

When something is weighted at the bottom, it is unlikely to fall over. Focusing your attention to your feet on the floor is like weighting yourself so you don't fall over. You instantly bring yourself into contact with the present moment. The sense of groundlessness eases off. The thoughts spinning off into the world of "what ifs" slow down. Whatever is going on is still there, but you are able to face it from a place of stability and strength.

the benefits of meditation

The practice of meditation is already well known for helping with a variety of issues we may be familiar with or have experienced ourselves. For example, meditation helps alleviate stress and anxiety, improves communication issues, helps bring greater clarity to our thoughts and actions, strengthens our concentration, increases self-awareness, and helps us to feel more objective about situations that are troubling to us.

The well-being benefits are enough for anyone to think, "I'll give it a go," but what marks this practice out in a world of ever-changing health fads is that meditation quietly works away in the background, ever reliable, and can be picked up with relative ease, without requiring hours of time or even considerable investment.

Meditation doesn't hand you the answers on a plate; rather, it allows you to come up with the answers for yourself. Meditation is like a friend who just sits with you while you come up with your own answers: you inevitably thank your friend for their help when, in fact, you came up with everything on your own. You just needed that space, that inner sanctuary, to discover what you already knew.

time for you

Taking time out for us is often at the very bottom of our to-do list; it may not even be a priority at all. It's far easier to relegate our needs to the bottom rung of importance, and yet it is vital that we do pencil in time for our own needs, even if that means taking a few minutes out of our day just to sit and breathe.

Meditation is simply the practice of being in the moment: allowing yourself the time to focus on a singular activity, whether you follow the rhythm and sound of your own breathing, become more aware of your presence and the sensations in your body, or maybe just observe your steps as you take a walk. It is that unique moment in your day when you allow yourself to pause for greater reflection and understanding, which helps calm and declutter the mind. We rarely allow ourselves that time and put enormous pressure on ourselves to be "doing" at every moment, be it working ever longer hours or making sure we keep up with the current trends and fashions so that the outside is looking perfect, leaving little if not any room for our inner life. You could say that meditation is taking care of the "inner business" of living, helping us maintain a good balance between the inner and outer aspects of our lives.

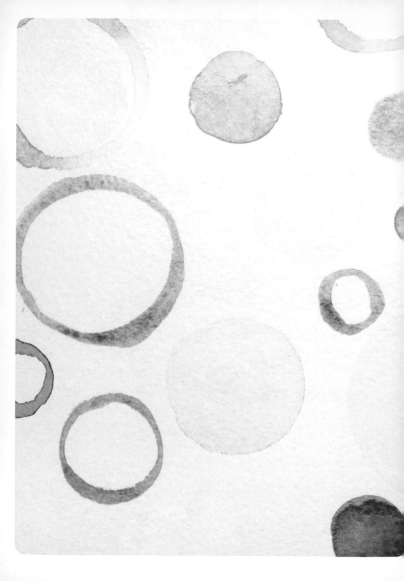

very little is needed
to make a happy life;
it is all within yourself,
in your way of thinking.

MARCUS AURELIUS

CHAPTER 3

MAKE IT HAPPEN

taking a risk

Have you the courage to let go of the person you think you are right now in order to find happiness? Are you brave enough to live life to the full? For most of our lives, we may choose to live within a personal comfort zone of familiarity and safety; in doing so we think we remain safe from harm and away from failure. But the truth is that the safer we feel, the more afraid we become, because doing something unfamiliar feels increasingly daunting. A very safe life can become an anxious life, lived within self-limiting boundaries. Happiness may become unhappiness because we are not living a life that is fulfilled. Interestingly, it is when we risk failure that we learn the most; and it is when we start to stretch ourselves that our potential for happiness increases.

what is your attitude to new situations?

Do you embrace new situations fully and worry about the consequences afterwards; or do you choose not to try because you don't want to risk failure? Whatever your attitude, decide on a new challenge and choose to behave in a way that is opposite to your usual behavior. If you are risk averse, just say yes to the opportunity; if you usually leap before thinking, decide this time to ask advice or create a plan. The new risk-taker may discover that she is better at thinking on her feet than she realized; the new planner may discover that when fully prepared, she can achieve even greater heights.

what role do you play?

Sometimes we are so attached to a particular view of ourselves that we don't realize that it is holding us back. What words do you use to describe yourself? Are you the shy one, the sporty one, the clever one, the one who is hopeless at x, y, or z? Where do the origins of those beliefs come from? Are they really true? What opportunities are you not taking because you can't see yourself in the role? How does it feel to try on some other labels for size, such as:

I have courage • I have talent • I have the tenacity to succeed
I am a dancer • I am a singer • I am good at sport
I am an attractive person • I am sociable • I am happy.

The brain appreciates clear direction and will fulfill your new instructions if you keep repeating them over a period of time.

BEING OUR BEST

There are several different kinds of happiness, but the hardest won are those moments resulting from extreme effort, where we have learned something new, achieved a long-term goal, done battle with ourselves or our environment—and won. Doing your best and achieving the outcome you hoped for reaps long-term rewards. It is a state of happiness well earned and well deserved.

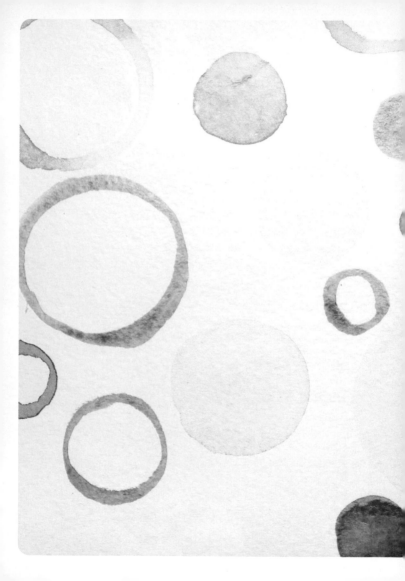

be fearless in the
pursuit of what sets
your soul on fire

letting go of fear

There are times in life when we need to risk all to gain happiness, while also letting go of some aspect that feels familiar. Strange as it may seem, sometimes the hardest thing to let go of is the safety blanket called fear. Fear encourages us to stay put, to remain risk-averse. It is the voice in your ear that tells you, "It's not worth the risk," and, "It's better not to try than to fail." By so not-doing, you are in danger of forfeiting the opportunity and living a life filled with regrets.

The pathways to happiness appear in many guises, and not all of them are immediately recognizable as ones you would want to venture down. They may look strange, too threatening, too full of obstacles, too far away from home, too frightening. But happiness is closely related to feelings of positive self-worth and achievement. We need to take calculated risks in order to grow and develop self-respect.

These key moments in life act as turning points that encourage us to take stock because there is a choice to be made, or something is about to change, and nothing will ever be the same again. It may be a milestone of achievement; a birthday that marks a new decade; a moment of loss and grief; or an opportunity that is simultaneously exciting and terrifying.

In these moments, we measure where we are against where we expected to be, and compare what we have achieved with what we originally dreamed of for ourselves. They are brave moments that challenge contentment and shake up the future.

Happiness is a large emotion, full of life. It doesn't thrive in situations where over-thinking stifles action, or where resentment and disappointment close the heart to the possibility of feeling joy. Somewhere between lost dreams and reality are thoughts you can dwell upon, steps you can take, and choices you can make that will dispel unwanted fears and turn potential regrets into opportunities for growth and change.

fear busters

The roots of fear lie in the mind and in our memory. Fear is the body's way of protecting us from real or perceived threat. Anxiety triggers the adrenaline response and increases blood flow to the heart, in preparation for "fight" or "flight." If you can identify your thought triggers, you can get to the source of the fear—and understand what makes you truly happy.

ask yourself:

• What are you frightened of? Is it a fear of something real, or something imaginary? (The mind cannot differentiate between the two.)

• What is motivating you to act and what might be holding you back?

• What do you have control over—so you can change it?

• What do you have no control over—so you will have to accept it?

• On a scale of 0 to 10, how happy will your decision make you?

• Will your decision lead you to step toward or away from further happiness?

Much has been written about the "comfort" zone—that familiar space we operate within from day to day; and the "stretch" zone—where we learn new skills and develop new competencies. With competence comes confidence, which boosts self-worth and self-esteem. Coach and trainer Bev James often reminds those who attend her courses that unless we find the courage to step into the stretch zone, we will be forever wondering what life might have held, if only we had been a little braver.

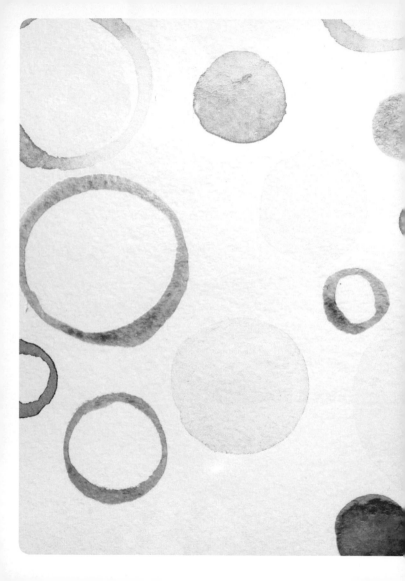

everything you've ever
wanted is on the other
side of fear.

GEORGE ADAIR

think like a lottery winner

If you were to win the lottery tomorrow, how would you feel? What would you do to celebrate? Would you invest your winnings, share them, spend them? After the initial euphoria passed, what do you think you would value the most about your home, your friends, your family—and the world? Would anything have changed in your life?

The lottery mentality is interesting because it encourages us to think in extremes. By pushing the limits of our imagination, we tap into another part of ourselves that tends to be restrained by daily commitments, habits of thought, and financial circumstances. It may not be possible to improve the material side of your life overnight—but you don't need to wait until you win the lottery to start becoming the person you would ideally like to be.

try asking yourself:

- What are you putting off doing "until the conditions are right" that you could start doing right now?

- What could you do for someone else that would make them feel as if it was their lucky day?

- In what ways are you already a lottery winner?

- What are the keys to unlocking your more adventurous side?

have some fun

Children have the right idea about life because they know how to play. They know what makes them happy and how to have fun! It doesn't matter how little they have in the way of props—they can have fun anyhow. We might tell ourselves that play is foolish or it's just for the kids, but having fun is essential not only to our well-being, but also to manifesting what we want (see page 135). Happiness, joy, and love are high vibrations. They fill us with life energy and make us feel alive! Remember, if something feels good, it is right for us, and it is meant to be and is part of our path. The universe attracts us to what we should be doing and having by dangling a "feel-good" carrot; it feels good because it is part of who we are. Feeling love, happiness, and joy is our natural intended state. When we feel joy, we are in "divine flow."

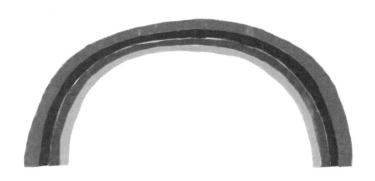

Think about these free sources of joy and see how you are affected by the mere thought of them. A real belly laugh, a genuine "I love you," a big, gummy smile from a baby, a breeze on your face, a cuddle, a sunset, a completed task, a thank you, a warm welcome, giving gifts, family, a cat's purr, the sea, friendship, a kiss. There are thousands more, but you get the idea. The key is to recognize what brings you joy. And when you know what it is, include it in your life every chance you get.

find your path

In order to feel more fulfilled in our lives, we need to find out what makes us happy and what it is that gives us that surge of excitement. The trouble is, finding out what we really want can also be rather difficult, as the thing we are looking for may seem intangible at times; we can sense that there is something more but we can't always put our finger on precisely what that is. Meditation can be used as a kind of sounding board to play around with ideas, dreams, and aspirations; your very own space to start building toward your goals.

Our path doesn't have to follow a set structure and can change to accommodate our needs. If we think about what we truly want for ourselves, we will likely come up with one or two ideas that we have not previously considered. This meditation will help you clarify both your immediate goals and your dreams for the future.

1 Find a comfortable place to sit. For this exercise, you can close your eyes or keep them open, just as long as you pick a specific point in the room on which to focus. Ask yourself the question: "What do I want to do?" You don't have to analyze it or think about it in great detail, just throw it out into the room. It can help to ask the question aloud.

2 Bring your attention to your breathing and allow yourself to ruminate gently on the question you have asked, without thinking too hard or wracking your brain for an answer. Just trust what comes up (even if at this moment you have drawn a blank) and remain firmly in the moment by keeping your breath as the point of focus. If we allow ourselves to be relaxed and open, we encourage inspiration to strike.

3 The answer may come up unexpectedly or further into the meditation. Try not to feel that the answer has to be perfectly in line with what you were hoping for. It doesn't have to be something on a grand scale, like your ultimate career objective; instead, it could be something more immediate, such as deciding that you would like to go traveling. It's good to remember that what we want is always changing and evolving, so don't be concerned if you find that your goals and objectives are different from what you originally thought.

4 When the answer comes to the fore, ask yourself why you haven't yet made strides towards achieving this objective; it may be due to financial reasons or time constraints, or perhaps you simply haven't given it much thought. Now is the time to think about what you could do to move toward realizing this goal for yourself.

5 The next step is to visualize achieving this objective; how do you feel now? Is there a sense of satisfaction? Do you feel content, exhilarated, relieved? If we get a sense of what the reality could potentially feel like, it then begins to take shape as an idea; visualization is that first step to realizing what we want.

This exercise can be used any time you decide you want to make a change, to help you ascertain what is most important to you right now.

do something today
that your future self
will thank you for

daring to be a beginner

When we are children, we learn new things all the time. Every new experience and skill stretches us, gives us confidence, and widens our world. However, as adults our learning often slows right down or even grinds to a halt.

As we become good at particular skills, we may specialize and even become an expert. As an expert we may feel we have a certain position to uphold and so we may be reluctant to jeopardize our status. Whether we are an expert or not, as adults we are often self-conscious and worried about making a fool of ourselves, so our default is not to do anything that is outside of our comfort zone.

Research has shown that the brain is much more plastic than previously thought and the potential for learning new things is always there—"use it or lose it" is just as applicable to the brain as to the physical body. So there is a physiological rationale for learning new skills, as well as a psychological one. If our life revolves entirely around work and our identity is defined by what we do, we become more vulnerable when things go wrong at work. Our very being is shaken.

However, if we can expand our interests and include non-work-related activities, we are building our confidence. It might seem scary and we may be anxious and nervous, but it is only when we move out of our comfort zone that we can grow. When we realize that we can do something even when we feel apprehensive at first, we realize that perhaps we can do other things, too. Learning new skills through different activities often brings us into contact with a different circle of people. This brings with it an opportunity to talk about non-work-related things and so really give ourselves a break.

Give yourself permission to be a beginner—let go of any expectations or agenda. Is there something you've always yearned to do? What would you like to try and learn?

the benefits of learning a new skill

• Learning something as an adult is a totally different experience from learning at school—you can study purely out of interest without an agenda. You could learn DIY, plumbing, sewing, cooking, a foreign language, art appreciation, fencing, squash, swimming, woodcarving, or how to play the harmonica—the possibilities are endless.

• Having a regular class after work gives you a reason to leave on time. Even if you're tired at the end of the day, using your mind or body differently is relaxing in its own way. Learning a new skill requires paying attention and focus, so this is a great way to switch off the work-mind.

• Certain activities, such as singing in a choir, actually reduce stress as we do them. Physical activities in particular are often stress busters. Kickboxing will give a healthy release to any stress hormones built up during the day. Qigong, tai chi, or yoga are also activities that focus on the body—and remember that when we focus on the body we get out of the head.

• If the weather permits, try an outdoor activity. Spending time outside, even in the city, connects you to the passing seasons and natural world and can give you a wider perspective.

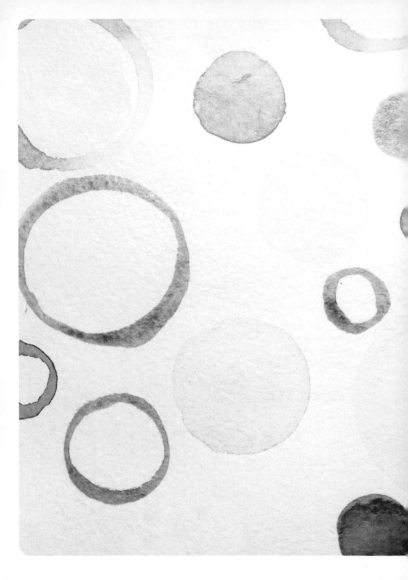

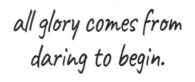

all glory comes from
daring to begin.

EUGENE F. WARE

look to the future

This particular meditation enables us to start planning for things to come by visualizing our future, giving us clarity in understanding our goals while remaining grounded in the here and now. For this exercise, you will need a notepad and a pen.

1 Get comfortable in your meditation area, gently close your eyes, and find your center by breathing gently, keeping your focus on the rise and fall of your chest. Focus on your breath for as long as you wish, as this helps calm and balance you before the visualization.

2 Allow yourself to be calm and, when you feel ready, in your own time, gently open your eyes, place the notepad on your lap, and write down your hopes and dreams for the future. They don't have to be in chronological order or have any specific correlation, just write down ideas, phrases, or even feelings that relate to what you hope to achieve. You can scrawl over the page in large letters, small letters, or even use illustrations if you are feeling particularly creative; whatever you do should represent your thoughts and feelings, uninhibited by your impulse to dilute your dreams in any way. This is not the time for modest thinking—really state your dreams with clarity and intent. Remember, this sheet of paper is for your eyes only.

3 Once you have filled the paper with your ideas and musings, spend the next few minutes simply looking over the page to get a sense of what you are pulled toward and what ideas and thoughts jump off the page; what is the dream you yearn for the most? Choose the one that you are drawn to, not the dream you think you ought to pick.

4 Close your eyes to return to the meditation. Focus on your breath and then, after a few moments, bring your chosen goal to the fore in your mind. Ask yourself a few questions in order to gain clarity on what it is you wish to achieve:

- Why have I chosen this particular ambition?

- What would it mean to my life if I achieved it?

- How can I achieve it? What steps do I need to take?

You don't have to answer all the questions in this one meditation session. This exercise could even be carried out over the course of a week, in which you give yourself the time to work through the questions.

WHY? WHAT? HOW?

5 Once you have asked yourself the questions, simply allow yourself to ruminate on those thoughts at your own pace. You might like to refocus on your breath and then, if an idea or thought comes up, make a note of it. Try not to analyze the thoughts or feelings, even if you think they appear silly or overambitious; whatever may come up, just allow it to evolve organically. Remember, everything that has ever been achieved started with an idea, so allow yourself the same time to think and create.

6 When you feel that you have come to the end of the meditation, sit quietly for a few moments. This allows the information to assimilate and you can look back on your notes later with fresh eyes.

DID YOU KNOW?

Although there are many different types of meditation, the end result is the common thread that ties the practice together. The aim is ultimately to find a deeper and clearer understanding of the self.

manifestation

Is there something missing in your life? What do you really want? Would you like more money, a new home, new job, or new love, or just to be happier? What if you can have anything you want, and you have the power within you to create it?

Well, you can create what you wish for. Being happy is your birthright. The universe is constructed so that once a clear request is sent out, the laws of the universe are instigated, and a result is guaranteed. A few simple guidelines have to be adhered to, and then anything is possible!

The energy that flows through everything flows through us, so we are linked to everything and everyone—we are an intrinsic part of the universe. And no matter how much or how little we know or remember this, we can all recognize and activate the universe's laws and creative forces. As human beings, we are already equipped with everything we need, but working with manifestation will get the process moving and help you reach your potential more quickly. All you need to do is ask— and it will happen.

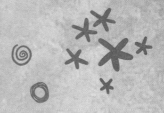

the manifestation process

We were each born with a special gift. This gift is our imagination—the ability to create something from nothing. Its impact is evident all around us. Someone, somewhere, has an idea or notion and, with a little effort, puts the idea into practice, creating something tangible. From the light bulb to the steam engine, everything is born of an idea, a thought, which manifests these great inventions and discoveries. And this same process can be applied to anything we might want or need in our daily lives. Whether it's a new car or a cure for an illness, the system is the same; the manifestation process begins with a single thought or idea. This thought may have been planted in us by the universe at just the right time, or may have lain dormant within us from before birth, just waiting to be awakened at the right moment. Either way, it only takes one thought to start the process.

A thought is given energy depending on how often it is used. The more we think a certain thought, the more energy we give it. It attracts other energies vibrating on the same or similar frequency according to its strength and nature (for instance, how much time the creator has spent thinking about it, and whether it has a positive or negative vibration). These other energies give the creator some kind of feedback about the potential outcome of the thought. For example, the creator might become aware of a similar experiment or breakthrough, or be offered help by another creator.

This is synchronicity at work—when the right information comes just at the right time. Fuelled by the confirmation that they are on the right track, the creator gives the thought or idea a great deal of thinking time. S/he imagines the outcome in different scenarios, but always imagines success. Related feelings fuel and drive the creator. The energy around the thought is now so vast, and the thought itself is so huge, that it is now more of a "belief." We base our beliefs on things that appear real to us: that is, things we can see and hear, or are told over and over again.

For example, you believe that grass is green, but who says so? Someone, somewhere, in the beginning made a decision that the color of grass would be called green. You might think this is a silly thing to say, but the point is we can believe things to be true just because we've been told enough times that they are. (After all, it may be possible that when one person sees green it is different to what another sees.)

The vibration then matches the belief and it becomes a reality. Every possible matching vibration is attracted to it, and the desired result is achieved. The thought or idea has become solid; we have fixed our attention on random subatomic particles and set them into the pattern we expected to achieve.

special guidelines

So, now you know that you can ask the universe for what you want, how do you do it?

• When you make a request to the universe, be clear. Say it repeatedly, visualize it, affirm it, think it, write it down, pray for it, and meditate on it, or do all of the above. Quite simply, the more energy or attention you give to your request, the more quickly it will be presented to you.

• Learn to think and act like the universe. You will understand why this is important when you consider how time-consuming it is to get a point across to a foreigner when neither of you has any understanding of each other's language. Sometimes it's possible, but it takes so long and there is much room for misinterpretation. Learn to speak the lingo and the problem is removed.

• To communicate easily with the universe—and therefore the highest of vibrations—we have to be vibrating as highly as possible ourselves, so when you are thinking about asking the cosmos for help, there is a frequency variation to take into consideration. This means you need to ask for help from a "feel-good" place.

why not give it a go?

1 Decide what it is you want. You don't have to decide on something forever—just decide what would be nice for now. You can adjust your request at any time.

2 Write down your wish, then tell yourself over again that it's already here. Speaking in the present tense takes your request out of your future and puts it into your present.

3 Visualize it over and over again. Start off by feeling a buzz if you can; get to a "feel-good" place and request from there. Believe your request will come to you, and it will.

4 Keep your list of wishes in a safe place, so you can go back to it and tick off requests as they happen.

let the universe do its job

When we recognize the ways we impede our journey to happiness, we can negate them. Often when there has been an absence of good things in our life, it's easier to believe that they won't come to us because we don't deserve them, or that happiness is something other people have. Another reason we veer off the path to our dreams is that sometimes we just can't see how what we really want can happen. Yet the universe can create miracles and has every possible option available to it, which we can't always foresee—for example, funding for a new business coming not from a bank loan, but from a charity, an unexpected inheritance, or an unclaimed insurance payout.

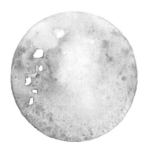

You don't have to know how your wish will be granted; you just have to believe that it will happen by having a bit of faith. Trust the limitless universe that can germinate seeds, bring perfect babies from a bunch of chromosomes, help night follow day follow night, and season follow season, to do its magic. Your dreams are no big deal for the universe. Just hand over your request and get on with your life, believing it will happen.

credits

text credits

© Anna Black: pages 12–21, 26–7, 36–43, 46–50, 52–60, 64–67, 70–73, 86–93, 96–97, 124–7

© Stephanie Brookes: pages 74–77, 98–100, 120–3, 130–3

© Joanne Gregory: pages 118–9, 135–41

© Rika Keck: pages 22–5, 28–33

© Sarah Sutton: pages 10–1, 78–83, 104–7, 110–3, 116–7

picture credits

© CICO Books

Trina Dalziel: pages 22, 37, 133

Clare Nicholas: 10, 11, 14, 15, 25, 38, 39, 40, 41, 43, 48, 49, 50, 52–3, 54–5, 56–7, 58–9, 60, 65, 97, 105, 107, 111, 113, 125

Rosie Scott: 1, 2, 3, 4, 5, 6, 7, 12, 13, 16, 17, 18, 19, 20, 21, 29, 46, 47, 81, 82, 83, 87, 90, 91, 93, 98, 99, 116–7, 118, 119, 130, 131

amaze
yourself today